Vatican II in Plain English

The Pastoral Constitution on the Church in the Modern World

Gaudium et Spes

Study Edition

ThomasMore®

Allen, Texas

NIHIL OBSTAT
Rev. Msgr. Glenn D. Gardner, J.C.D.
Censor Librorum

IMPRIMATUR
†Most Rev. Charles V. Grahmann
Bishop of Dallas

January 6, 1997

ACKNOWLEDGMENT
Scripture quotations are adapted from the New Revised Standard Version of the
Bible, copyright 1989 by the Division of Christian Education of the National
Council of the Churches of Christ in the USA. Used by permission. All rights
reserved.

Cover design: Bob Shema
Cover illustration: Karen Malzeke-McDonald

Paraphrase Text by Bill Huebsch and Paul Thurmes
Study Edition by Bill Huebsch and Jack Gargiulo

Send all inquiries to:

Thomas More Publishing   Toll Free   800-264-0368
200 East Bethany Drive   Fax   800-688-8356
Allen, Texas 75002-3804
Printed in the United States of America

Vatican II in Plain English
The Council   ISBN 0-88347-349-6
The Constitutions   ISBN 0-88347-350-X
The Decrees and Declarations   ISBN 0-88347-351-8
Slipcase (Set of all three books)   ISBN 0-88347-348-8

Constitution Booklets
The Dogmatic Constitution on the Church   ISBN 0-88347-369-0
The Dogmatic Constitution on Divine Revelation   ISBN 0-88347-370-4
The Constitution on the Sacred Liturgy   ISBN 0-88347-371-2
The Pastoral Constitution on the Church
   in the Modern World   ISBN 0-88347-372-0
Set of all four books   ISBN 0-88347-368-2

1 2 3 4 5   01 00 99 98 97

CONTENTS

*This book is dedicated
to the memory of
Father Karl Rahner, S.J.*

How the Study Guide Works

This study guide is designed to help people enter into the document itself. It is in two parts.

Part A is for people or groups wanting only a brief introduction to the document. About twenty minutes is required to complete Part A, making it useful for the opening prayer and study period at parish leadership groups and other gatherings where time does not allow a longer period of study. For individual students, this approach is also helpful for a quick review of the document.

Part B assumes the work of Part A has been completed and goes further. It is meant for those wanting more depth in their study. About an hour is required for Part B, making it useful for classroom use or for individual users wanting a more thorough view of the document.

In both these parts, the option of viewing the video documentary *(The Faithful Revolution: Vatican II,* Thomas More, 1996), exploring the resources on the CD-ROM *(Destination: Vatican II,* Thomas More, 1996), and reading the original document is always encouraged. Also, opening and closing the study period with prayer and undertaking this study in light of each week's liturgical readings from Scripture provide a faith link which seems essential.

There is always a danger in undertaking too little a study of something. One does not become an expert on Vatican II with a cursory, twenty-minutes-per-month reading of the documents. The goal of Part A is not, therefore, to make us experts. The goal is to introduce us to the council's outcomes by providing us with a brief look at them in order to lay a groundwork for further study and reflection.

The hope and dream of this program is that all the faithful of the Church—laity, religious, and clergy—will become familiar with this material so that they will be better equipped to pass on the faith and help animate the world with the Christian Spirit. Its dream is that all the faithful will become more active and well informed ministers of the Church. Its dream is the dream of Pope John XXIII himself. May we recognize that, in the council's work, God is acting in our midst, sending forth the Spirit to renew the face of the earth!

PART ONE: THE CHURCH AND HUMANKIND'S VOCATION

BREAKING OPEN THE PREFACE AND CHAPTER ONE
(ARTICLES 1–22)
THE DIGNITY OF THE HUMAN PERSON

This section of the document turns its attention to the whole of humanity. The Church can best provide meaningful answers to life questions by reading the signs of the times, it says. The Church offers the world a positive view of the human person. In the depth of human nature, we find God. Our conscience is our most secret core and sanctuary. We are most free when we listen to our inner voice.

Part A

Read this chapter aloud one article at a time, pausing to complete the discussion in Part A. As you read, underline key passages. Talk together about the elements that you noticed.

For example, read article 1 and discuss some of the joys and hopes, tragedies and anxieties that all people face in today's world.

Conclude Part A by discussing: How does the light of the Gospel help you celebrate these triumphs or face these tragedies?

Part B

When you have completed Part A, go on to discuss these questions:

What are the best ways to help people respect human dignity?

What are some of the things that rob people of human dignity?

How would you describe today's search for meaning and spirituality?

PARAPHRASE TEXT

Preface

1 "The joy and hope, the grief and anxiety
    of the people of this age,
    especially those who are poor
    or in any way afflicted:
        this is the joy and hope,
            the grief and anxiety,
            of the followers of Christ."
Indeed, nothing genuinely human
    fails to raise an echo in their hearts.
The Christian community
    is, after all, a community of women and men
    truly linked with humankind and its history,
        bearing a message of salvation
        intended for all people.
2 This council, therefore,
    having already looked in depth at the Church itself,
    now turns its attention on the whole of humanity.

We want to state clearly our understanding
    of the presence and function of the Church
    in the world of today.
For the world is the theater of human history,
    its energies,
    its tragedies,
    and its triumphs.
The Christian vision is that the world was created
    and is sustained
        by God.
It was freed from the slavery of sin by Christ.
It is now being re-created and brought to its destiny
    under the Holy Spirit.
3 We now offer to the world
    the honest assistance of the Church
    in fostering human harmony which is our destiny.
In this, we follow our teacher, Christ,
    who came to give witness to truth
        and to serve and not be served.
People today are troubled and perplexed
    by questions about their lives in the world,
    about their place in the universe,
    about the meaning of individual and collective work,
        and about the purpose and nature
        of being human.
We now wish to enter into dialogue
    with the whole human family about all this.
We will clarify these questions
    in the light of the Gospel
    and offer the human race the saving resources
        of the Church.
Our entire subject is humankind,
    men and women:
        whole and entire
        with body and soul,
        with heart and conscience,
        with mind and will.

Introductory Statement

4 In order to proceed here,
    we must understand the world in which we live,
        its expectations,
        its longings,
            and its often dramatic ways.
In language understandable for each generation,
    the Church should be able to give
    a meaningful answer to questions people have
        about life:
        both now and after death.
We must, in other words, read the signs of the times.

One of those signs
    is the profound and rapid change
    that is everywhere.
Riding on the intelligence of the human race,
    the creative energies of people
    have produced unprecedented social transformation.
As we might expect,
    this transformation has also brought
        serious difficulties.
Never has the human race enjoyed more wealth,
    yet a huge number of people are tormented
        by poverty, illiteracy, and want.
Never has there been such human freedom in the world,
    yet new forms of social and psychological slavery
        also make their appearance alongside it.
Never has the world been so close to the brink of unity
    and interdependence,
    yet new and opposing camps
        threaten this possibility.
There is even the frightening prospect
    of a war of total destruction!
Never before has the drive for a better world
    been more on the minds of men and women,

yet there is not a corresponding spiritual advancement
    to give it meaning and guidance.
As a result, many people are burdened with uneasiness
    even as they enjoy the benefits
      of modern life.
We humans must respond to all of this;
    indeed, we cannot escape doing so.

5 Today's spiritual hungers result, in part,
    from a much more scientific approach
    to understanding the world.
Technology is transforming the world,
    not to mention outer space!
And to a certain extent, the human intellect
    is even beginning to control time:
        the past by means of historical knowledge,
        the future by means
          of projecting and planning.
Likewise, advances in the social sciences,
    including biology, psychology, and others,
    bring us hope of improved self-knowledge.
At the same time,
    the human race is now considering the regulation
    of its own population growth.
History speeds along on so rapid a course
    that one can scarcely keep abreast of it,
    and we humans have now passed
      from a rather static understanding of reality
      to one much more dynamic
        and evolutionary!

6 By this very fact, local groups,
    such as families, clans, or villages,
    are rapidly being transformed.
Ideas and social conditions that have lasted for centuries
    are quickly being replaced in our time
    by new concepts of social organization.

City living is much more common today,
    for example,
    and even rural places have citylike lifestyles.
New and incredibly efficient media
    make connections around the world possible
    so that styles of thought and feeling
        can be known worldwide
        that were once limited in their scope.
Migration is increasing as well,
    and this creates a socialization
    that doesn't always include personal relationships.
And while what we describe here is true
    in advanced nations,
    it is rapidly becoming more and more true
        worldwide.

[7] So much change calls traditional values into question,
    especially among young people
    who are not satisfied to wait until adulthood
        to take their role in this dynamic.
Hence, the handing down of teachings and traditions
    is more difficult than ever before.
Religion is also affected, of course,
    by this new world movement.
On one hand, superstitious and magical views of the world
    are eradicated by science and knowledge,
    which purify faith in the unseen God.
On the other hand, growing numbers of people
    are abandoning religion
    in favor of science or humanism.
Evidence of this disturbing trend
    is found in literature,
        art,
        the humanities,
        history,
        and even in civil law.

8 All these modern developments,
     coming so rapidly and disorderly,
     intensify imbalances within the human person.
One's intellect, for example, may be thoroughly modern,
     while one's theory of meaning is more traditional,
          and no joining of the two seems possible.
Or one's concern for practicality and efficiency
     is in tension with one's moral conscience.
Or the demands of collective existence
     conflict with one's need for personal thought,
          or even contemplation.
Furthermore, the family is in tension
     with pressures on it from many sides:
          population control,
          economic realities,
          or social demands.
Likewise, tensions emerge among nations
     when some are so wealthy and others so poor.
All of this leads to mistrust,
     division,
     and hardship,
          and humans are at once the cause
          and the victims of it all.

9 For the first time in history,
     many believe it is possible and desirable
     that the benefits of modern culture
          can be extended to everyone.
And those who do not yet have these benefits want them,
     especially
          the world's starving people,
          women,
          workers,
          and farmers.
There is also a movement for a universal community
     in which persons can live a full and free life.

In all of this,
> the modern world is both powerful and weak,
> capable of noble deeds or foul ones,
> in the path of freedom or that of slavery.

Modern people seek new levels of meaning today
> precisely because of the unleashed powers
>> of modern life,
>> which can either serve us or destroy us.

10 The modern condition is rooted
> in the nature of human life itself.
> boundless in ambition yet limited,
> attracted to many things,
>> but forced to choose among them,
>> often choosing those things
>>> known to be harmful.

Many who choose practical materialism
> do not even give this matter thought!

Others are weighed down by unhappiness
> and do not have the emotional wherewithal
>> to consider it.

Still others believe human effort alone
> is sufficient to order society
> and bring meaning and peace to humankind.

And some believe there is no meaning in life
> to begin with.

Yet there are those, increasing in number, who ask:
> "What is the human person?
> What is this sense of sorrow,
>> of evil,
>> of death,
>> which continues to exist despite progress?
> What victory have we won in these times,
>> and at what cost?
> What can we expect from life,
>> what can we offer to it?
> What follows our earthly life?"

We in the Church firmly believe
    that the Light of Christ can illumine our search.
Beneath these many changes and developments
    is an unchanging and loving God,
    and we now speak of these matters
        in order to cooperate in finding the solution
        to the outstanding problems of our age.

Part One: The Church and Humankind's Vocation

11 We begin our inquiry with the People of God,
    which believes it is led by the Holy Spirit.
This People of God,
    this human family of which we are part,
    makes careful inquiry into the events,
        needs,
        and desires of this age
    to find authentic signs of God's presence here:
Who are we humans, anyway?
    What does society need today to be better?
    What do human actions throughout the world mean?
People are waiting for answers to these questions,
    and by this inquiry, it will become clear
    that the Church and the world
        render service to each othe,r
        for the mission of the Church is religious
        but is also supremely human!

Chapter One
THE DIGNITY OF THE HUMAN PERSON

12 Everyone on earth believes
    with nearly unanimous opinion
    that the human person is the center and crown
        of the earth.
But what is the human person?

There are divergent views among people about this,
    some exalting the human person
    as the measure of all things
        and others debasing human nature
        to the point of despair.
We take a positive view of the human person,
    based on the words of our Scriptures,
    expressed in the Book of Genesis,
    that God created us in the divine likeness
        and was pleased with the outcome.
We understand ourselves, furthermore,
    to be essentially social creatures,
    created from the beginning to have companions.

13 But there is more.
The human person quickly attempted to separate
    from the Creator
    and chose to oppose God,
        according to our scriptural stories.
Human experience agrees with this:
    for when we examine our hearts,
    we do indeed find an inclination toward
        disrupted relationships
        and darkness.
We find ourselves split within ourselves,
    caught in a dramatic struggle of good versus evil,
    light versus darkness.
And into this situation,
    we believe God sent Jesus Christ,
    the Light of the World,
        to strengthen us with grace
        and to free us from the darkness.

14 For the human person,
    although composed of both body and soul,
        is a unified, whole person,
        not divided.

We are obliged to love our bodies and, indeed,
    the whole material world,
      for it is created by God too.
Nevertheless, it is often there,
    in the material, physical realm,
      that we find inclinations toward darkness.
So we must probe our human nature to its depth
    to find our souls,
      and when we do, we will not be mocked,
        for there in the depth of our hearts,
          we also find God.

15 We can conclude from this plunging into our depths
    that in some ways
    we humans surpass the material universe
    and share in the light of the divine mind.
We have made great progress in many arenas,
    using our talents,
      and we continue to win enormous victories
        in science, technology, and the liberal arts.
Nonetheless, we continue to search
    for penetrating truths
      and find them!
We can look beyond observable data
    and employ the wisdom
    that perfects our intelligence,
      and it is this wisdom
        that we now need so badly
          or the world may perish.
Wise men and women must come forth
    to lead us in this age,
      and they may well come from less developed places
        where wisdom often thrives.
This wisdom leads us to desire goodness and truth.

16 In the depths of our conscience,
    we detect a law

which we have not laid upon ourselves
    but which we must obey.
Its voice, ever calling us to love
    and to do what is good and avoid evil,
    is heard at the right moments in our lives.
It speaks to our hearts: "Do this; shun that."
For this law, written into our very hearts,
    is from God.
Our very dignity comes from observing this inner law,
    and by it we will be judged.
Conscience is our most secret core and sanctuary.
It is where we are alone with God,
    whose voice echoes in our depths.
The voice we hear will always,
    in a variety of ways,
    call us to love God and neighbor well.
By being faithful to it,
    we are joined with all of humanity
    in a great human search
        for truth
        and for genuine solutions
            to the vexing problems
            of modern life.
It is clear from what we are saying here
    that we must be faithful, then,
    to that inner voice,
        that "divine guide" in our souls,
        and not allow our clarity to be dulled
        by repeated acts that are contrary to love.
We must not allow our souls
    to be nibbled away by acts of hate and selfishness.

[17] The key to this is freedom.
Authentic human freedom does not mean
    "doing whatever we please."
Rather, it flows from attentive listening
    to our conscience,

as well as in doing what our conscience directs.
Such free choices will always be fully human ones
and will not result from impulsive actions
or from external rules.
We humans have the potential to spontaneously
choose Good
with God as our inner guide.

18 It is in the face of death
that all this is brought into sharp relief and focus,
for death eventually claims us all
and none of our technology can stop it.
And even if we could prolong life,
we would still be possessed of an innate sense
of a higher life in the divine love.
For we believe that God created us for eternal life,
where the wholeness we lose through sin
will be restored
because of the mercy of Christ.
Faith, therefore, fills thoughtful people with hope
and unites them with all who have already died.

19 For our lives flow from the creative energy
of this Faith
and return there as well
in an intimate and eternal linkage.
Because we believe this link with God
is vital for human happiness and fulfillment,
we want to examine atheism in all its forms.
We consider it one of the most serious problems
of this age.
There are many kinds of atheism,
some very subtle forms and others more blatant.
There are those, for example,
who expressly deny the existence of God at all
but others who simply argue
that we can know nothing at all about God,

whoever God may be.
Others believe that all truths can be explained by reason
    or even that there is no absolute truth to explain
        in the first place!
Some hold humanity in such high regard
    that they have left only an anemic faith in God,
    though they may not deny God outrightly.
And still others simply have no religious stirrings,
    no desire to ask these questions at all.

20 Modern atheism confuses human freedom
    with our relationship to God
    as though the two cannot coexist.
It claims that men and women will be freed
    by economic gains
    or social advancement.

21 But we believe and have always taught
    that the true nature of humans
    is to be joined with the divine life force,
        that real freedom comes in this.
We continue to teach this,
    and we assert firmly that any other approach
    robs human persons of their dignity
    and offers them only economic or social solutions
        to situations demanding more!
22 We believe that hoping in eternal life
    does not diminish human life here and now
    but propels us to live with great nobility
        because when we die we take with us
        the love we have in our hearts.
Without this hope, indeed,
    the riddles of life and death,
    of guilt and of grief,
        go unresolved
        and people often succumb to despair.

Our lives remain unsolved puzzles,
    especially when major life events unfold for us.
We come to understand ourselves
        more and more
        only with the wisdom of God.
So the remedy that we apply to atheism is twofold:
        the proper presentation of the Church's teaching
        and well-lived Christian lives.
People will see us believers,
        as they did the martyrs and others in the past;
        they will see our unity and charity,
                and come to believe themselves.

For us Christians,
        the truth and meaning of our lives
        is wrapped up in the mystery of Christ,
                the Incarnate Word of God.
In Christ, the riddles of sorrow and death
        take on meaning,
        the divine presence is made profoundly clear,
        and we find the energy and power to live fully.
In Christ, we become capable of being fully human,
        sharing in the full divinity,
        divinity made flesh,
                working with human hands,
                thinking with a human mind,
                acting by human choice,
                and, above all, loving with a human heart.
What greater love do we need?
        What greater truth?
The mystery of the human person
        is centered in this divine core,
        revealed through Christ,
                and stirring us to full humanity.

BREAKING OPEN CHAPTER TWO
(ARTICLES 23–32)
THE COMMUNITY OF HUMANKIND

This section of the document reinforces this basic truth: Whoever loves God must love neighbor. We love our neighbor by working for justice and freedom. The document encourages us to always defeat whatever violates human dignity. We are also encouraged to respect all people, even those who think differently than we do.

Part A

Read this chapter aloud one article at a time, pausing to complete the discussion in Part A. As you read, underline key passages. Talk together about the elements that you noticed.

For example, article 26 describes the common good. Discuss how you or your parish adds to and supports the common good.

Part B

When you have completed Part A, go on to discuss these questions:

What are some of the things that build unity in your family? Your neighborhood? Your parish?

What are some practical steps you take to understand and respect people who think differently than you? Where does the line stop between respecting others and avoiding what is false?

PARAPHRASE TEXT

Chapter Two
THE COMMUNITY OF HUMANKIND

23–24 There is a growing interdependence
among people today

which is based on the many technological advances
    that are obvious to everyone.
But this interdependence reaches its perfection
    only in growing human relationships,
    not merely scientific ones.
For God, we believe, desires that all people
    become one family
    with love for God and neighbor as the basis.
We cannot separate these two:
    whoever loves God must love neighbor
        or the love is false.
    Jesus said as much himself.
It is obvious how important this is
    as we come to rely more on each other
        and grow in unity.
Because of Jesus' prayer
    "that all may be one as we are one,"
    new horizons are now opened for us,
    implying that we will reach our true destiny
        only by pursuing such oneness
        with each other.
25 So we humans, in order to fully discover ourselves,
    must donate ourselves to one another in love.
This aspect of human nature,
    the social aspect,
    suggests strongly that the advance of society
    depends on individual persons progressing first.
After all, the whole purpose of social organizations
    is to make human life more noble.
This social nature of which we speak
    makes it clear that the progress of the human person
    and the advance of society
        go hand in hand.
After all, the whole purpose of social institutions
    such as the family,
        political parties,
        labor organizations,

and even the churches,
is to enhance our lives
as human persons.
Indeed, some of these social institutions
arise from the very intrinsic nature of being human.
The family is one of these,
as is the political community.
Other social institutions are created by us
to serve our needs,
and our participation in them is more voluntary.
And both of these are on the rise today,
increasing both in number and influence.
Even though this is true, however,
it is also true today
that men and women are often diverted
from doing good
and spurred toward doing evil,
and the cause of this is the very social order
in which they live
and into which they have been born.
There are natural tensions in any social plan,
especially economic life,
political organization,
and various social groups.
These are the tensions that often yield
to a breakdown in human nature,
based on human pride and selfishness
which contaminate these social activities.
Sin results.
Sin can be overcome
only by steady effort with the help of grace.
26 There is a condition in human life that we call
the common good.
By this term, we refer to that set of conditions
of human life,
economic, social, political, and others,
which, taken together,

makes it possible for us
to become all we are created to be,
to reach our human fulfillment.
Various social groups
approach the common good differently
and must take each other into account, therefore,
if all humanity is to achieve it.
We recognize with increasing awareness today
that there is a fundamental human dignity
which must be in place for the common good
to be possible in the first place.
This fundamental human dignity is universal
and unchanging,
based as it is in our created nature.
It leads us to say that everyone must have
food, clothing, and shelter;
the right to choose a state of life freely;
the right to found a family;
the right to education, employment,
a good reputation, respect,
and appropriate information;
the right to follow one's own conscience;
the right to the protection of privacy
and to rightful freedom,
even in matters of religion.
Our point is becoming more clear here:
all social organizing must be for the benefit
of the human person,
and it requires constant improvement.
It must be founded on truth,
built on justice,
animated by love,
and growing in freedom.
And we realize that in order for this to be true today,
substantial adjustments in attitude
and abundant changes in current society
will have to take place.

But we believe that God's Spirit
    continues to hover over this growth in human order
    and to renew the face of the earth.
And, furthermore, we believe that it is rooted
    in the very heart of men and women
    to seek increasing dignity,
        and not to sink into darkness.

[27] In practical terms, this means
    that everyone must consider his or her neighbor,
        without exception,
        "another self."
Each person must take into account first of all
    the life of each other person
    and the means necessary to live with dignity.

It must not be with us as it was with the nameless rich man
    who saw Lazarus bleeding and hungry,
    without this dignity of which we speak here,
        and ignored him.
Remember what happened?
    Lazarus rested in the bosom of Abraham and Sarah
    while that rich man lived on in isolation,
        selfishness,
        and ignorance:
            hell.
In our times, this means we have a special obligation
    to make ourselves the neighbor of every person
        without exception
    and to actively assist them when we meet them
        in the path of our lives.
This includes old people abandoned by all,
    foreigners in our midst,
    refugees,
    children without parents,
    and hungry people.

All of these, when we see them and hear their cry,
    disturb our conscience
    and remind us of Jesus' teaching in Matthew 25:
        "As long as you did it for one of these,
          . . . you did it for me."
And not only that.
We must also work to defeat
    any force opposed to life itself,
    such as any kind of murder,
        genocide,
        abortion,
        euthanasia,
        or willful self-destruction.
We must work to defeat
    whatever violates human dignity,
    such as mutilation,
        mental or physical torture,
        coercion of the will,
        subhuman living conditions,
        arbitrary imprisonment,
        deportation,
        slavery,
        prostitution,
        the selling of women and children,
        and disgraceful working conditions.
All of these poison human society,
    doing harm to both those afflicted by them
    and those perpetrating them.
They are, in short, a supreme dishonor
    to the Creator God.

28 We should also have respect and love
    for those who think differently than we do
    in social,
        political,
        or even religious matters.
In fact, the more deeply we understand others,
    the more we can dialogue with them,

seeking understanding.
This is not to say we should accept
    untruth as truth
    or meanness as goodness.
But the people whom we believe to be in untruth
    are dignified nonetheless,
    and we teach that only God can make judgment
        in the end.
God alone is the searcher of the human heart,
    and we should not make judgments
    about the internal guilt of anyone.
To the contrary,
    we are taught by Jesus to love
    even those we consider our enemies.

29 Every person has a soul and is created in God's image.
    All people are of the same nature and origin.
Having been offered a unique relationship
    of sonship and daughtership with God by Christ,
    all likewise have the same divine calling.
There is, therefore, a basic equality of all human persons
    regardless of social or cultural background,
        race,
        gender,
        color,
        language,
        or religion.
All discrimination should be overcome
    and eradicated,
    and we regret that so many human rights
        are not being honored around the world,
        especially for women who are not free
            to choose a husband freely,
            to embrace a state of life,
            to acquire an education,
            or to enjoy cultural benefits
                equal to men.

As we have made clear above,
    human institutions, both private and public,
    must labor to enhance the dignity and purpose
        of all women and men.

30 A purely private sense of morality cannot exist
    in this day and age
    because of the interdependence we have
        on one another.
Each of us must not only fulfill our human call
    to live justly and with love
    but must also work to insure that social institutions
        are more fair.
Each of us contributes to the common good
    when we use our abilities
    in this way.
We should pay our just share of taxes,
    obey social laws,
    and conduct our business honestly.
We should operate our industry with an eye to
    the protection of human health around us.
It even comes down to obeying speed limits
    so that those around us are not in danger.
31 In sum, we call on everyone to consider it
    his or her sacred obligation
    to esteem and observe social needs.
If all do, a truly new and more humane society
    will be available to all.
For this to happen,
    education must be widespread,
    especially for youth of every background.
Likewise, neither destitution nor sumptuousness
    is our aim
    but the building up of the common good.
Hence, the desire to take part in organizing society
    should be encouraged for everyone,
    and we offer special praise for those nations

that allow the fullest possible participation
in governance and public affairs.
32 Once again we point out that God did not create humans
to live in isolation
but in community.
We are not individuals set side by side
without bonds or links,
but rather, we are bound together
as a single people,
with one common inner principle, the Spirit.
This communal nature of ours
finds its fullest expression in Jesus Christ,
who lived in radical human fellowship.
The lifestyle, friendships, and social engagements of Jesus
point the way for us:
we are to live as one Body,
members of one another,
rendering mutual service to each other
based on our gifts.
And this communal solidarity in Christ
must be increased steadily
until we live fully with God as one family.

BREAKING OPEN CHAPTER THREE
(ARTICLES 33–39)

HUMAN ACTIVITY THROUGHOUT THE WORLD

This section of the document describes how human activity flows
from people and benefits people. In fact, human advances are a
sign of God's grace. The document says that the law of love is
the basic law of human growth. Making the world a better place
makes us more noble and prepares us for eternity.

Part A

Read this chapter aloud one article at a time, pausing to complete the discussion in Part A. As you read, underline key passages. Talk together about the elements that you noticed.

For example, read article 36 and discuss: Do modern advances create a gap between faith and science?

Conclude Part A by giving specific examples of how science brings you closer to God.

Part B:

When you have completed Part A, go on to discuss these questions:

What do you consider the most important scientific, medical, and technological advances in your lifetime?

How have these advances benefited you? Other people?

What are some risks of ignoring God in a fast-moving, scientific world?

In what ways is the world a better place now than twenty-five years ago?

PARAPHRASE TEXT

Chapter Three
HUMAN ACTIVITY THROUGHOUT THE WORLD

33 Men and women have ceaselessly labored
    to improve their lives,
        using their talents and hard work to do so.
Today that work is paying off more than ever,
    and nearly every aspect of human life
    has come under our control
        through science and technology.
Little by little the worldwide human family
    is realizing that it is indeed just that,
    a family united by common concerns.

The result of this is that many phenomena
    which were once attributed to divine power
    are now fully understood to be of human making.
But all of this leaves us with certain nagging questions
    about life, meaning, and the end goal of it all.

The Church stands in the midst of these questions
    and offers guidance,
      without having all the solutions.
The Church can offer principles for proceeding
    and wants to add to the human journey
    the light of truth
      so that we do not wander in darkness.
34 Christians are convinced that the triumphs
    of human endeavor,
    the wonderful advances of society,
    and the monumental efforts
      to produce a better world
      are completely in accord with God's will.
It is the very mission of the human person
    to understand and use the benefits of creation
      to the good of all.
Therefore, in everyday life,
    as well as in more dramatic ways,
    when we work for our livelihoods,
    God is present, unfolding ongoing creative work.
Hence, far from thinking that such human advances
    are in opposition to God's desires,
    we are convinced they are a sign of God's grace.
We therefore say with confidence
    that we are not hindered from improving the world
      by the Christian message
      but, on the contrary, bound to do just that.

35 Human activity, to be sure,
    flows from people and benefits people.
When someone works,

he or she alters things and society,
    but he or she also develops his or her very self.
In a word, she or he grows,
    and this growth is more valuable
    than the external wealth it produces.
A person is more precious for what she or he is
    than for what he or she has.
Likewise, then, we also believe
    that whatever is done to obtain justice,
        to establish a broader solidarity,
        and to make living conditions more humane
            is more valuable than technology.
We can, therefore, draw this principle from our thinking:
    all human endeavor is of God
    when it allows men and women
        to pursue their created purpose
        and follow it to fulfillment.

36 Many modern people seem to fear
    that a closer bond between human activity
        and religion
        will work against independence in science.
We have sometimes even been led by certain Christians
    to believe that faith and science oppose one another
    but we do not agree with this at all.
The deep realities of society and science
    are deciphered by us little by little,
    and this gradual discovery of the universe
        is our natural instinct
        and also, we believe, God's will.
Whoever works to learn about the world in this way,
    even if they are unaware of it,
        is nevertheless being led by the hand of God
            in whom everything continues in being
            and finds its ultimate meaning.
If such methodological study is carried out
    in a genuinely scientific way

and follows moral norms,
> then it is of God.

But if the scientist denies the place of the divine
> in his or her work,
> > it is false,
> > > because apart from the Creator,
> > > > creation no longer exists.

When God is forgotten, human life loses meaning.

37 We know from our Scriptures and our history
> that we humans seem bound to wrestle constantly
> > with selfish desires.

When these self-centered ways of behaving emerge in us,
> they threaten the peace and security of our race,
> and this is especially true today.

Hence, the world has not yet become a place
> of true sisterhood and brotherhood.

So we must wrestle with dark desires
> made manifest in a spirit of vanity and malice,
> and it at this very point that the Church
> > offers us a helping hand.

In order to overcome this tendency toward darkness,
> we must come to Christ.

By this we mean that our motives and actions
> are made more pure and perfect
> when we realize that everything we have
> > comes from God
> > and is intended for us to share.

Such an attitude makes us free and humble:
> free to receive everything
> and humble to know its source is not ourselves.

38 For Christ has shown us the way of love,
> and the law of love is the basic law
> of human growth, development, and transformation.

To those who believe in divine love,
> Christ has shown that the hope of a world

based on love
is not a foolish hope.
This hope must be pursued in common, everyday life
as we "lay down our lives" for one another,
having learned to do this from Christ
and believing that doing so
will lead all to a glorious shared life.
Christ is present in the midst of this,
providing the energy we need,
arousing the desire for good in us,
animating our hearts,
and purifying our noble longings
for human solidarity.
This work is done by Christ in the hearts of people
by the power of the Holy Spirit.
This Spirit first arouses in us
the desire for a better world
but also encourages the best and most noble
of our sentiments
so they will be used toward this end:
to make Christ present.
And this divine presence of Christ
is nowhere more profound
than in the Eucharist itself,
where indeed the natural elements
of bread and wine
are changed into a meal of solidarity!

39 All of this is so important to us
because of our belief
that the world in which we now live
is but a foreshadowing of what is to come.
We believe that the betterment of this world
is God's will and desire,
for it makes us humans more noble
and prepares us for an eternity
on this same path of wholeness
and holiness.

BREAKING OPEN CHAPTER FOUR
(ARTICLES 40–45)
THE ROLE OF THE CHURCH IN THE MODERN WORLD

This section of the document explains the interdependent relationship of the Church assisting the world and the world assisting the Church. The Church believes that religion and everyday life are part and parcel of each other. The document says that both realms advance the reign of God.

Part A

Read this chapter aloud one article at a time, pausing to complete the discussion in Part A. As you read, underline key passages. Talk together about the elements that you noticed.

For example, read article 43 and discuss the idea that when we neglect our temporal duties we neglect our spiritual duties. Give personal examples of how some of the temporal duties you perform also have a spiritual dimension.

Conclude Part A by discussing how your parish has helped you balance your temporal and spiritual duties.

Part B

When you have completed Part A, go on to discuss these questions:

What are some important factors that foster positive dialogue between the Church and the world?

What are some riddles of life posed by today's world?

Do you think the world is on the brink of greater or less unity?

What is the Church's greatest contribution to the modern world?

Paraphrase Text

Chapter Four
The Role of the Church in the Modern World

⁴⁰ Everything we have said about the human person,
  about human dignity,
  human community,
  and the meaning of human activity
    now serves as the foundation
    for what we wish to say here.
We will speak about the place of the Church in the world
  and the dialogue between them.
As we make our comments now,
  we also base them on what we have said
  about the nature of the Church
    as a sign to the world
    of the presence of God.
The Church, as we have already said,
  emerges from God's love for us
  and God's desire that we form a divine family
    during our lifetimes.
The Church is thus a leaven and a soul
  for human society
  and, as such, that part of the Church
    which is found on earth, here and now,
    and that part which is to come
      in heaven later,
      penetrate each other.
This is most evident in the Church's task
  of elevating and healing the dignity of being human
  and insisting on this point,
    even in the face of darkness.
The Church offers deep meaning and purpose
  to those who hear her word
  and contributes greatly to making the human family
    more human!

This is a two-way relationship:
    the Church assists the world,
    and the world assists the Church
        interdependently.
And this applies to the Roman Catholic Church
    but also to other church bodies
    who have the same goal.
[41] We now intend to set forth certain principles
    for the proper fostering of this mutual exchange
    between the churches and the world.

Members of the human family today
    are on the road to a more thorough development
        of their personalities
    and to a growing discovery and absolute claim
        on basic human rights.
These ultimate goals of being human
    are written on the heart;
    they are part and parcel of life,
        the fundamental meaning of existence,
        and the innermost nature of humankind.
We believe that only God can lead us
    to this truth;
    only God provides an answer to the riddle of life.
The Church is a stable force
    that steadfastly maintains human dignity
    even in the face of fluctuating trends in society
        regarding the value of life
        and the human body.
No one can protect humans from exploitation
    better than those who speak for God,
    and today that is the Gospel of Christ,
        entrusted to the Church.
The Gospel has a sacred reverence
    for the dignity of conscience
    and its freedom of choice.
It announces and proclaims the freedom

of the sons and daughters of God,
and it rejects wholeheartedly all forms of slavery,
    internal and external,
    which result from human mistakes.
By virtue of this Gospel,
    the Church proclaims the rights of humankind.
It acknowledges and affirms those movements today
    that support and foster these rights,
    desiring to penetrate them
    with the spirit of the Gospel
        so that we do not wander into the belief
        that our rights are ensured
        only when we are also free of divine law.
Indeed, divine law is most natural to humans
    and without it the dignity of the human person
        will perish.

42 The Church is not tied to any specific system
    of government,
    economics,
    or social order.
The purpose that Christ gave the Church
    is, indeed, only a religious one.
But out of that mission
    can come a light and clarity to guide others
    and the energy of love to serve as their center.
As a matter of fact, the Church can and should
    undertake certain works herself,
    such as assisting the poor and suffering.
We see an evolution in the world today
    toward unity
    which pleases us because the innermost nature
        of the Church
        is the promotion of unity.
And since the Church is committed to no single system
    of governance,
    she can bridge them all,
    serving as catalyst.

We therefore urge all women and men
    to put strife and division aside
    and live together in peace.
This council looks with great respect on all that is true,
    good,
    and just in social systems everywhere.
The Church is willing to promote and assist these systems
    and has no fiercer desire than to develop freely
    under every system that grants recognition
        to the basic rights of person and family
        and the demands of the common good.

43 We Christians believe that these times and this life
    will ultimately end in an eternal dwelling place.
Nonetheless, we also believe that life in this world
    and in these times
    must be lived nobly, fully,
    and with attention to our day-to-day obligations.
And we also believe that religion and everyday life
    are intimately and indissolubly linked,
    part and parcel of each other.
        We cannot divorce what happens in religion
        from how we live our everyday life.
Simply put, there is no split between faith
    and everyday life.
Jesus himself repeatedly warned against
    dividing life and religious belief in this way.
So did the prophets of the time before Christ!
Therefore, let there be no false distinctions
    between one's professional and social life
    and one's religious life.
If you neglect your temporal duties,
    you also neglect your spiritual ones!
It behooves us Christians, then,
    to become skilled at our trades,
    to pay attention to developing expertise,
        and to use it wisely.

Laypeople ought to follow their well-formed consciences
    so that the divine law
    is lived out in everyday life,
        looking to priests for spiritual nourishment,
        but not imagining they have all the answers!
And when faithful people disagree,
    and that will certainly be the case,
    do not presume to speak for God or the Church
        but try to enlighten one another
        through honest discussion and charity,
        always earnest in your search for truth.
In this way, laypeople, guided by their pastors
    who are guided by their bishops,
    will indeed animate the world
        with a Christian spirit.
Pastors and bishops, therefore,
    must remember that their daily conduct
    reflects the Gospel and greatly influences others.
We believe the Church has always been
    a faithful lover of Jesus
    and an everlasting sign of salvation.
But we are also aware that some of her pastors,
    as well as laypeople,
    have not always been faithful to this love;
        some have failed to live out the very message
        that they are bound to preach!
However history judges them,
    we should be aware of this
    and work to improve such failings,
        purifying and renewing ourselves
        so that the Light of Christ
        can indeed shine through us all!

44 As we have just described it,
        the Church can add greatly to the modern world,
        but the modern world can also benefit
            the Church.

The progress of science
and the treasures hidden in various forms
of human culture
reveal new roads to truth.
The Church wants to speak in the language of the people
and needs the help
of those versed in varying specialties
to do this.
Because change occurs so rapidly today
and thought patterns differ so widely,
the Church needs to increase the activity
of adapting herself to this age.
To do this, she calls for help
from the people living in the world
who understand these times so well.
In this way, the Church is enriched
by the development of human social life,
and all those who promote the values of the Gospels,
however that is done,
benefit the mission of the Church as well.
The Church has a visible social structure
which is a sign of its unity in Christ.
Because of this social nature,
we know that whoever contributes
to the development of humankind on the level of
family,
culture,
economic and social life,
or national or international politics,
when they order these
according to the plan of God,
also contributes to the life of the Church herself.
Even those who persecute the Church
in some ways assist her.

45 In all this,
the Church's assistance to the world

and the world's assistance to the Church,
   there is one single intention on our part:
       that God's Reign be established
       and that all men and women
           be made whole.
For the end of everything is life in God;
   for us this means life in Christ.
Christ is the answer to our longings,
   the center of the human race,
   the joy of every heart.
Enlivened and joined in Christ's Spirit,
   we recognize that, indeed,
       Christ is the Alpha and the Omega,
       the beginning and the end of all that is.

PART TWO: SOME PROBLEMS OF SPECIAL URGENCY

BREAKING OPEN
PREFACE AND CHAPTER ONE
(ARTICLES 46–52)

FOSTERING THE NOBILITY OF MARRIAGE AND THE FAMILY

This section of the document talks about the partnership of married life and love. There are some modern trends that hinder this partnership. However, the example of married couples joined in authentic sexual love, harmony of mind, and mutual holiness gives great witness to the mystery of love.

Part A

Read this chapter aloud one article at a time, pausing to complete the discussion in Part A. As you read, underline key passages. Talk together about the elements that you noticed.

For example, read article 47 and discuss: What are some concrete ways your parish fosters good marriages and family life?

Conclude Part A by discussing: What important message about marriage and family life do you convey to others?

Part B

When you have completed Part A, go on to discuss these questions:

What is the meaning of today's divorce rate?

How do children contribute to making the family holy?

How are parenting skills best acquired?

PARAPHRASE TEXT

Part Two: Some Problems of Special Urgency

Preface

46 Having spoken in the council
about the dignity of the human person
and the work that all people are called to do
both as individuals and members of society,
we now turn our attention
to five specific questions:
marriage and the family;
human culture;
social, political, and economic life;
bonds among the nations;
war and peace.
We hope to speak of these under the Light of Christ
so that Christians may be properly guided
and all humankind enlightened
as we search for answers
to complex questions.

Chapter One
FOSTERING THE NOBILITY OF MARRIAGE AND THE FAMILY

47 Marriage and family life
are the bedrock of a healthy human society,
and we are pleased to see ways
in which these "partnerships of love"
are fostered today.
But there are also ways in which they are hindered,
such as polygamy,
divorce,
so-called free love,
excessive self-love,
the idealizing of pleasure,
and the illicit use of birth control.

It is also disrupted by
 modern economic conditions,
 social and psychological influences,
 the demands of civil society,
 and problems resulting from population growth.
In each of these cases,
 an anguish of conscience results for many
 which is terribly painful and disruptive.
By reflecting on key points
 (though not on all related matters),
 we wish to support marriage and family life.

48 The partnership of married life and love,
 first of all,
 is created by God
 and rooted in sexual union
  when there is permanent,
   personal,
   and mutual consent.
Once agreed to, this bond is no longer purely human
 but now takes on a divine nature
 and is oriented toward having children
  and forming a family.
The two married partners render mutual service
 to each other
 through their sexual love and daily life,
  leading them to total fidelity
  and unbreakable oneness.
Love of this sort wells up
 from the fountain of divine love
 that flows from Christ
  so that authentic married love
  comes from God.
It is for this reason that the Church
 treats marriage as a sacrament,
 a sign of God's faithful love of us,
 and a source of grace for the partners.

The love present in marriage is, then,
    really divine love
    expressed through sex and mutuality
    and lived out in the raising of the family.
Children, likewise, contribute in their own way
    to making their parents and the entire family holy.
Families thus share an interdependence,
    providing support in hard times
    and sharing everyday life.

49 The love that a married couple shares
    is expressed and made perfect
    through sexual intercourse,
        of which the Scriptures speak glowingly
        and which unites human and divine
            in mutual giving and bliss.
This is not mere eroticism,
    which ultimately fades,
    but involves the whole person
    in faithfulness and richness
        otherwise not known to humans.
Supported by mutual fidelity
    and made holy through the sacrament of matrimony,
    this love continues as the couple is faithful
        in both mind and body,
        in good times and in bad.
It therefore excludes either adultery or divorce.
Children should be taught about this
    so they, too, can enter marriages that are holy.
50 Marriage has several ends,
    none of more or less account than the others.
Very important among them is the task of transmitting life
    and educating those
    to whom it has been transmitted.
In this, parents cooperate in creation,
    a divine activity,
    and must enter into this thoughtfully.

They should take into account those already born
    and those foreseen,
        considering both the material and spiritual conditions
            of the times
            and of their family's state.
They then consult the interests of the family group,
    of temporal society,
    and of the Church's teachings.
The parents should, then, ultimately make this judgment
    in the sight of God,
    following their conscience,
        enlightened by divine law,
        and guided by the Church.
Thus, parents sometimes stop having children
    and yet maintain their love,
        for the purpose of marriage is not solely tied
            to procreation.
The mutual love of the spouses, too,
    must be embodied in a right manner;
    it must grow and ripen.

51 This can be very difficult if sexual loving is ended
    in order to prevent conception
    and can endanger the bond
        as well as the quality of family life.
We reject wholeheartedly a solution to this
    that involves the taking of life
    through abortion or the killing of infants.
Since the transmission of human life
    is not merely a human activity,
    sexual intercourse and responsible conception
        must be harmonized.
Decisions made toward this end
    will be based on objective standards
        that reflect divine love.
Catholics are not allowed to use methods of birth regulation
    that are disapproved of

by the teaching authority of the Church.
How all of this will be understood in our day and age
    has been handed over to a special commission
    which will report soon to the pope,
        and for that reason,
        this is all we will say here about it.

52 The family is a school of deeper humanity
    and needs the communion of minds
    and joint decisions of spouses
    as well as the cooperation of the children
        to be maintained.
Having the father present is essential,
    and allowing the mother her domestic role
    is also needed,
        though this should not undermine
        the legitimate social progress of women.
Children should be prepared for independence
    and not forced into marriage.
Hence families are the foundation of society,
    and governments should support them.
Those skilled in science, too,
    can support the regulation of births
    and peace of conscience,
        especially those in medicine,
        biology,
        social science,
        and psychology.
Organizations outside the family can also offer support,
    especially for children and spouses.
And, finally, spouses themselves,
    joined in authentic sexual love,
    harmony of mind,
    and mutual holiness,
        witness to the presence of God
        and the mystery of love.

BREAKING OPEN CHAPTER TWO
(ARTICLES 53–62)

THE PROPER DEVELOPMENT OF CULTURE

This section of the document examines the changes taking place in social and cultural life. The accompanying issues are many. The Church offers basic principles so that faith and culture can work together. The document also acknowledges the tension between the growth of a new culture and its consistency with the heritage of tradition.

Part A

Read this chapter aloud one article at a time, pausing to complete the discussion in Part A. As you read, underline key passages. Talk together about the elements that you noticed.

For example, read article 56 and discuss: How important is it to you to be well informed about the news of the world? How does the news connect to the Good News of the Gospels?

Conclude Part A by discussing: What effort do you make and what sources do you use to reach a better understanding of truth, goodness, and fairness?

Part B

When you have completed Part A, go on to discuss these questions:

What aspects of modern culture give you a better understanding of goodness, beauty, and fairness?

What aspects of life as portrayed by mass media do you embrace or reject?

Are people more responsible for each other in today's world compared to the world of twenty-five years ago?

Do you consider yourself optimistic about modern advances?

Do modern advances enrich or diminish faith?

PARAPHRASE TEXT

Chapter Two
THE PROPER DEVELOPMENT OF CULTURE

53 The cultivation of the goods and values of nature
 are the basis of the authentic human person.
People live in both culture and nature.
There are, of course, numerous cultures,
 each having a historical aspect
 as well as a social dimension,
 a sociological sense,
 and a unique ethnic character.
All culture implies "community living"
 and includes patterns for sharing wealth,
 various ways of laboring,
 of language,
 of religious practice,
 of forming customs,
 of making laws and courts,
 of advancing the arts, sciences, and beauty.
54 Because of all the changes that have taken place recently
 in social and cultural life,
 we can actually call this a "new age"
 in human history.
The enormous growth of natural, human, and social science
 not to mention communications and technology,
 has paved the way
 for a modern refinement of culture.
Critical judgment has been shaped to a fine edge
 by the exact sciences, for example.
Human behavior is explained more fully
 by psychological research.
Historical studies throw new light on our past,
 helping us see how changeable
 and evolutionary the world is.
All over the world, customs are more uniform,

lifestyles are similarly urban,
and new ways of thinking and using leisure
    are everywhere.
Thus, little by little, a more universal form
    of human culture is developing
    through which the unity of humankind
    is being fostered.
55 We are increasingly aware
    that we are the authors of this new culture,
    that we are directly responsible for it
    and will live under it.
There is a new humanism in the world today
    which defines us first and foremost
    as responsible for each other.

56 All of this raises some difficult new questions
    for us today.
How can we continue to increase exchange among cultures
    while at the same time
    maintain the identity of the small community,
    preserve ancestral wisdom,
    and save the uniqueness of each people?
How can the vitality and growth of a new culture
    harmonize with the heritage of tradition?
How can branches of knowledge shoot out so quickly
    while at the same time we undertake
    a necessary synthesis of them
        so men and women can still grow in wisdom
        through contemplation and wonder?
How can all women and men on earth share somehow
    in the new technology?
And finally, how will we maintain the independence
    that culture claims for itself
    without developing a humanism devoid of God?

57 Here are some principles that we can follow
    to begin to offer answers to these questions.

First of all,
    faith and culture work together
    with many of the same aims and goals.
The fact that faith points people toward divine life
    does not diminish people's attention to human life,
        because the two are intimately linked.
Most aspects of culture elevate the human family
    to a more sublime understanding
        of truth, goodness, beauty, and fairness.
Even though there is a temptation in science
    and under modern scientific thinking
    to doubt everything not observable,
        nonetheless it also prepares us
        to remain close to God.
Furthermore, modern advancements
    provide many positive values,
    including the study of science,
        fidelity to truth in this study,
        teamwork in technology,
        international solidarity,
        the role of experts in helping all,
        and an eagerness to improve
            the human standard of living.

58 Second, the Church is not bound
    to any particular culture or period of history;
    human culture and religious culture advance
        as one reality.
The Good News of Christ
    mixes with life and human culture
    to combat and remove error and evil,
    to purify and elevate the morality of peoples,
    and to assist spiritual qualities to blossom.

59 Third, the purpose of culture
    is the benefit of humans,
    the good of the community and of society.
It is the role of culture to develop

the human spirit of wonder,
    understanding,
    contemplation,
    the formation of personal judgments,
    and the development of a religious,
        moral,
        and social sense of self.
Toward this end,
    the rights of the individual
    and the needs of the community
        are both safeguarded
        within the limits of the common good.
Cultural development requires that a certain freedom
    be in place,
    freedom to search for truth,
        voice one's mind,
        and publicize one's beliefs.
Public authority should make this possible everywhere.

60 Because it is possible today
    to liberate most people from ignorance,
    Christians have the urgent duty to provide education
        wherever it is needed.
This will make it possible for a fuller participation
    in cultural life for many people
        who otherwise would not be included,
        especially country people and laborers,
        as well as women.
Regarding women especially,
    everyone is responsible to ensure
    that their specific role in cultural life
        is fostered.

61 With so much new knowledge today,
    almost no one can grasp it all
    and unify all aspects of human understanding
        in his or her thinking.
Nonetheless, it is essential that we maintain a view

of humans as whole persons,
including intellect, will, and conscience.
Taking advantage of increased leisure
for reading,
sports, and physical activities,
time with family,
and travel
will enrich people and help them reach
an emotional balance.

62 It has proven difficult sometimes
to harmonize culture with the Church,
but it is necessary to do that.
Recent studies and findings of science,
history,
and philosophy
raise new questions about life
and demand new theological investigations.
Furthermore, theologians are invited
to find more suitable ways
to communicate doctrine to the people
of their times.
The Deposit of Faith or revealed truths are one thing
but the manner in which they are expressed
is another.
Pastors can employ psychology and sociology
to more effectively bring faith to life.
Literature and the arts can elevate men and women
to new planes of understanding
about our place in history
and the meaning of these times.
The Church should give recognition, therefore,
to these arts, including new artistic forms,
and introduce them into the sanctuary
when appropriate.
Christ's faithful can thereby live in closer union
with their neighbors

if religious practice and morality keep pace
    with science and its theories.
Theological inquiry should seek a profound understanding
    of revealed truth
    without neglecting close contact with its own times.
Laypeople ought to be trained in the sacred sciences
    and some will deepen these studies
    by their own labors.
And, finally, everyone possesses
    a lawful freedom of inquiry and thought
    and the freedom to express their minds humbly
        but with courage
        about those matters
            in which they enjoy competence.

BREAKING OPEN CHAPTER THREE
(ARTICLES 63–72)

SOCIO-ECONOMIC LIFE

This section of the document offers eight basic guidelines for economic development. These guidelines emphasize the need for everyone to work for justice and to contribute to the peace of the world and the prosperity of humankind.

Part A

Read this chapter aloud one article at a time, pausing to complete the discussion in Part A. As you read, underline key passages. Talk together about the elements that you noticed.

For example, read article 72 and discuss: What is the connection between working for justice and achieving world peace?

Conclude Part A by discussing: Which of the beatitudes do you most vigorously try to carry out in your daily life?

Part B

When you have completed Part A, go on to discuss these questions:

What can a Christian bring to his or her workplace that will benefit others?

How can one person make a difference in creating a better world?

PARAPHRASE TEXT

Chapter Three
SOCIO-ECONOMIC LIFE

63 Once again in the arena of economics,
    we declare that the dignity and wholeness
    of the human person
        must be honored as the center of focus.
As we have noted in other areas of human activity,
    the economic life of women and men
    is characterized by
        an increasing domination of nature,
        closer and more intense ties among citizens,
        more mutual interdependence among nations,
        and frequent government intervention.
At the same time, there has been great economic progress
    which has made it possible to provide
    for the increasing needs of the human race.
Still, there are reasons for anxiety today.
Many people are so captivated by their economic lives
    that they seem nearly hypnotized by it,
    both in wealthy nations as well as poorer ones.
We have the ability to make everyone on earth
    economically comfortable,

yet so often a minority is served
 and a majority suffer.
Hence, luxury and misery rub shoulders,
 and while the wealthy are able to choose
 among competing economic goods,
  the deprived have almost no such choices
  and live in subhuman conditions.
There often seems to be a lack of balance even within a nation
 among various industries:
  farming,
  manufacturing,
  and service industries.
And the imbalance among nations
 threatens the peace of the world!
Because all of this is true,
 this council now turns its attention
 to this important and dynamic human activity
 to reinforce certain principles
  and set forth certain guidelines
  to assist in economic development.

64 First and foremost,
 technical progress must be fostered
 to make it more possible to provide for all.
Along with this, a spirit of initiative,
 an eagerness to create and expand enterprises,
 the adaptation of methods of production,
 and the hard work of all who engage in production,
  all of these must be fostered too.
But here is the principle:
 the purpose of this is not to make anyone rich;
 it is not to give some the means of dominating others.
The purpose of this is to be in the service of all humans
 in terms of their intellectual,
  moral,
  and religious lives.

Economic development must, therefore,
>   be carried out according to clear moral standards
>   so that God's desire for humans is realized.

65 Not only that, but second,
>   economic development must be under the control
>   of the human family, working together,
>   not left to the sole judgment of a few
>   who possess economic or political power.
Within a nation, the citizens must decide these matters
>   together among themselves.
Among nations, all affected parties should participate.
In all cases, people and their rights come first
>   and production is the secondary aim.
Citizens have the right and duty to contribute
>   to economic development and production
>   according to their skills.
Those with the means to do so
>   should not let their investment funds lay fallow
>   but should put them to use to employ others!

66 Third, and very importantly,
>   vigorous efforts must be made as quickly as possible
>   to reduce or remove
>   the immense economic inequalities
>   that now exist.
The demands of justice require this.
In particular, farmers and country people
>   must be helped to receive their just compensation.
Immigrant or migrant workers should be welcomed
>   and discrimination against them avoided,
>   and they should not be treated as mere tools
>   of production.
And in all places,
>   leaders should take care to provide suitable work
>   for all who are capable of it.
In situations where industry is changing quickly,
>   as in the use of automation, for example,

care should be taken that workers still have labor.
And those who are unable to work,
    who are old or infirm,
    should also be cared for.

67 Fourth, it is our clear principle
    that human labor as a part of production
    is superior to other elements
        of economic life.
It is ordinarily by her or his labors
    that a woman or man supports herself or himself.
It is also how humans serve one another,
    join together in common efforts of charity,
    and become partners in God's unfolding creation.
Jesus himself was such a worker.
Hence, everyone has a duty to work,
    and society has a duty to make work available
    and to be certain that wages are fair.
Toward this end and in keeping with principles of justice,
    working conditions must be suitable and safe,
    and economic slavery must be ended.
In fact, the work life should be adapted
    to the needs of the persons doing it,
    especially mothers and the aged.
Finally, workers should be able to develop as persons
    through their labors
    and to have ample leisure time
        for family, cultural life, and prayer.

68 Fifth, workers themselves should share
    in the decision making that affects their workplace
        as well as their industry.
Freely founded labor unions are a human right
    and provide an orderly way
    for workers to participate
    as long as their means is peaceful
        and conflict is resolved through negotiation
        and without resort to violence.

Workers have the right to elect their own representatives
    to these unions
    and to be part of them without reprisal.

[69] Sixth, the earth and all it contains
    are meant for all to share fairly.
Whatever forms of ownership are followed,
    attention must always be paid
    to this universal purpose,
    and all the goods of the earth
        should benefit all the people of the earth.
Hence, we are bound to come to the relief of the poor
    and to do so not only out of our leftovers
        but out of our very subsistence.
Today, the poor number among the majority
    so that we call on all people and nations
    with the means to do so
        to undertake a genuine sharing
        of their goods.
In less advanced societies,
    customs that no longer work
    should be updated so all are cared for.
Social services that support the family
    should be encouraged everywhere
    but not so much that the citizens
        form negative attitudes toward society.

[70] Seventh, toward this end,
    the distribution of goods and services
    around the world should not be limited to charity
        but should be directed toward helping
        people find employment
        and sufficient income.
This will require economic planning
    so that today's needs are not met
    at the expense of tomorrow's.
Furthermore, underdeveloped nations
    should receive special attention
    in economic planning.

Special care should be taken that such nations
    not suffer when money values decline.

71 Eighth, it is important for people to own the resources
    of their nations
    and to have some control over material goods.
Such private ownership
    or another form of private dominion
        over material goods
        provides a necessary independence.
It adds incentives for carrying on one's work
    and constitutes a prerequisite for civil liberties.
This is not to be seen to be in conflict
    with necessary public ownership
    of certain resources
        that serve the public good.
In situations where the majority own most of the land
    while the minority have none or very little,
    steps should be taken toward balance.
Often in these situations, the workers
    are paid too little to live on
    and lack decent housing
        while the owners and merchants
        take all the profits.
Some people live in virtual slavery as a result of this,
    and all gains in culture and dignity are impossible.
Reforms are to be instituted in these cases
    and may include the redivision of land,
    cooperative enterprises,
    or educational assistance to people
        to help make them more productive.

72 In closing this discussion of economic life,
    let us say that Christians who work for justice
    and take an active role in economic development
    are making a great contribution
        to the peace of the world
        and the prosperity of humankind.

They help permeate the world
    with the spirit of the beatitudes
    and grow in love as they work for justice.

BREAKING OPEN CHAPTER FOUR
(ARTICLES 73–76)

THE LIFE OF THE POLITICAL COMMUNITY

This section of the document deals with the nature of politics, which is to foster the common good. Even though the Church and political systems are independent, the Church is called to teach social doctrines and to make the human community more noble.

Part A

Read this chapter aloud one article at a time, pausing to complete the discussion in Part A. As you read, underline key passages. Talk together about the elements that you noticed.

For example, read article 73 and discuss: What do you consider to be some basic truths about the nature of government?

Conclude Part A by discussing: What are the best ways for you to generously serve others? To foster justice?

Part B

When you have completed Part A, go on to discuss these questions:

Is there a human instinct for freedom? What sustains that instinct? What diminishes it?

What are the things that help people strive for peace?

PARAPHRASE TEXT

Chapter Four
THE LIFE OF THE POLITICAL COMMUNITY

73 Changes are taking place today
   in how people are governed,
   and these include a growing awareness
      of the rights of minorities
      and of people's desire for freedom,
      freedom of assembly,
         of common action,
         and of religion.
There seems to be a broader spirit of cooperation
   taking hold around the world
   based on people's inner sense of justice,
      goodness,
      and the common good.
The best way to achieve a political life
   that serves people
   is to foster an inner sense of justice,
      generosity,
      and service of others.
We also want to strengthen basic beliefs
   about the nature of politics
   and about the proper limits of governments.

74 Acting alone, individuals or families
   are not sufficiently able to establish
   all that is needed for a fully human life.
Hence, we group together
   to provide for those conditions
   in which people can become their fully human,
      created,
      graced selves.
Authority in this common enterprise
   is a good thing and very much needed

to prevent people from fighting
　　as they pursue their own needs.
Such authority should function more as a moral force
　　than as a tyrant.
Hence, the political community exists for the sake
　　of the common good,
　　not for its own sake,
　　and when it is legally established in a nation,
　　　　citizens are bound to obey it.
If such political authority exceeds it bounds
　　and violates the rights or dignity of anyone,
　　then citizens are bound to defend themselves
　　　　against such abuses.
Whatever form of government is chosen in a nation,
　　it should make people more civilized,
　　　　peace-loving,
　　　　and full of desire for the common good.

75 Political systems should act without discrimination
　　and allow all citizens the chance
　　to participate freely and actively in forming a state
　　　　and choosing leaders.
Citizens, therefore, have a duty to vote,
　　and leaders are to be praised for stepping forth.
A system of law is also a good thing
　　when it protects rights
　　and furnishes the state with order and support.
But we should be on guard against granting government
　　too much authority
　　or seeking too much from it,
　　because that weakens the sense of responsibility
　　　　on the part of individuals,
　　　　　　families,
　　　　　　and groups.
If individual rights are temporarily suspended
　　during an emergency,
　　they should be restored very quickly.

Citizens, for their part, should be loyal to their country
    but not blind to the needs of the rest of the world.
They should be aware that there will be differences
    about how best to govern
    and enter into the public debate with a good heart.
Those who are suited for it
    should enter the art of politics
    without thought of personal gain
        or benefit of bribery.
Such leaders should oppose
    injustice and oppression,
    oligarchy or arbitrary use of power,
    and intolerance for diversity.

76 We must never confuse the Church
    with the political community
    nor bind it to any political system.
In fact, the political community and the Church
    are mutually independent and self-governing.
The Church's contribution is to introduce love and justice
    into society, not to govern it.
But it is also the Church's legitimate work
    to preach the faith in freedom,
    to teach her social doctrines,
    and to discharge her duty among people
        without hindrance.
The Church also has the right to pass moral judgments
    when the salvation of souls is at stake,
    for it is the Church's task to reveal,
        cherish,
        and ennoble
    all that is true,
        good,
        and beautiful
    in the human community.

BREAKING OPEN CHAPTER FIVE
(ARTICLES 77–90)

THE FOSTERING OF PEACE AND THE PROMOTION OF A COMMUNITY OF NATIONS

This section of the document connects the reality of peace with justice and love. Weapons are not a safe way to keep peace, the document says. Rather, peace is born of mutual trust between nations. The document emphasizes the role of cooperation between nations, whether wealthy or developing nations, as an essential part of human fulfillment.

Part A

Read this chapter aloud one article at a time, pausing to complete the discussion in Part A. As you read, underline key passages. Talk together about the elements that you noticed.

For example, read article 77 and discuss: What is your dream for peace?

Conclude Part A by discussing: In what part of your dream for achieving peace are you most involved?

Part B

When you have completed Part A, go on to discuss these questions:

What are some basic requirements for world peace?

Is violence a growing trend in your neighborhood? Schools? Country?

Do you consider the arms race a treacherous trap or a safeguard for all humanity?

What is your responsibility to those who are poor?

Paraphrase Text

Chapter Five
The Fostering of Peace and the Promotion of a Community of Nations

77 "Those who work for peace
   shall be called children of God"
   according to the Gospel of Matthew (5:9),
   and, indeed, in our day, these words
      shed new light on the human family's
      growth toward full development.
For we live in a time of war
   and the threat of war,
   and we are in a great human crisis.
We wish to cooperate with all people of goodwill
   to help establish a solid, lasting peace on earth.

78 Peace, we believe, is not merely the absence of war.
   Nor is it reduced to a silent, cold standoff
      where the parties remain armed.
   And it is not an outcome of dictatorship.

What is it, then?
   Indeed, what is "peace"?

Peace is a harmony built into human society
   by God, the divine Founder of all life,
   and it is a direct outcome of justice.
Such a peace is not attained once and for all
   but is constantly built up
   as people control their passions
      and governments remain vigilant.
But even this is not enough.
   For peace is the fruit of love as well.
It cannot be obtained and safeguarded
   unless men and women freely and trustingly
   share with one another their inner spirits and talents.

It is based on a firm determination to respect others,
 and to live lives of sisterhood and brotherhood.
Without such love, peace absolutely cannot prevail
 in our time.
For all of this flows from the peace of Christ,
 who first loved us
 and dedicated himself for us.
We urge all Christians, therefore,
 to join with all peacemakers in the world
 to plead for peace and bring it about.
We praise those who renounce violence
 and find other ways to settle disputes
 where fairness for all is assured.
We dream of the day when we will say with Isaiah (2:4),
 "They shall beat their swords into plowshares
  and their spears into pruning hooks;
  one nation shall not raise the sword
   against another,
  nor shall they train for war again."

[79] Despite this great dream of all people,
 savage warfare goes on all over the world,
 in fact, more savage than ever before.
Having considered all this,
 we in this council remind everyone
 first and foremost
  about the permanent, binding force
  of natural law,
  which is the law written in our very hearts.
Any action that deliberately conflicts with this law
 or any command ordering someone else to do so
  is criminal.
Blind obedience will excuse no one from this.

Among the actions which fall into this category,
 that is, which conflict with natural law,
 is any methodical extermination of an entire people,

nation,
    or ethnic minority.
No case can be made for such an action!
    It is always horrendously wrong!
Those who oppose such actions
    are highly praised.
International agreements to make military activity
    less inhumane
    should be strengthened and obeyed.

Now, on the subject of war,
    it clearly still exists on earth
    and, therefore, governments cannot be denied
    the right to legitimate defense when attacked;
        indeed, governments have a duty
        to protect their citizens.
But it is one thing to defend oneself or one's nation
    and another to move offensively against others.
All who volunteer for armed-service duty
    should think of themselves as agents of peace,
        security,
        and freedom.

80 We undertake an evaluation of war today
    with a new attitude
    because of the presence of weapons
    of total destruction.
Therefore, we hereby condemn total war completely,
    and following the teachings of Pope John XXIII
    in *Pacem in Terris*
    and Pope Paul VI at the United Nations,
        we issue this declaration:
Any act of war aimed indiscriminately at the destruction
    of entire cities
    or of extensive areas
        along with their populations
    is a crime against God and humanity itself

and merits absolute
and unhesitating
condemnation!
What is so unique about this situation
is that world events might unfold on their own
in such a way that someone may decide
to use such a weapon.
In order to help prevent this from happening,
we bishops of the entire world
urge all world leaders to consider
the awesome responsibility that is theirs
when their nations possess such weapons.

81 We also realize that such weapons,
based on modern science
and capable of total destruction,
are amassed with the thought in mind
that having them will deter an enemy
from attacking in the first place.
Many regard this as an effective way to keep peace.
We believe, on the contrary,
that this is not a safe way to keep peace at all.
The so-called "balance" that results
is unsure and unsteady,
and the threat of war only increases
as the number of weapons does.
Furthermore, while vast fortunes are spent
to purchase and build these weapons,
the poor continue to starve,
disagreements among nations are not healed,
and the world lives in terrible anxiety.
We say it again: this arms race is a treacherous trap
for all of humanity
and one that injures the poor
to an intolerable degree.
Let us work together to seek another approach,
one more worthy of the dignity of humanity.

If we fail to do this,
    we do not know where the evil path
    on which we tread
        will lead.

[82] Peace, then, must be born of mutual trust between nations
    rather than a doubtful outcome of their fear
        of one another's weapons.
We commit ourselves to work for the day
    when war, all war,
        can be completely outlawed
        by international consent.
In the meantime, let us move toward disarmament,
    not unilaterally but in every nation.
Many world leaders are now working
    to end war,
    and we commend you!
It is time to put aside purely national interests
    so that the whole community of humankind
    can find peace together.

The basis for this is in each person's change of heart
    as we regard the entire world
    and those tasks that we can perform in unison
        for the betterment of all people.
Peace will not come until hatreds end;
    until contempt for others ends;
    until distrust,
        unbending ideologies,
    and divisions
        cease.
The Church now takes its stand in the midst
    of these anxieties,
    which are felt in every nation of the world.
We intend to continually say to all:
    Now is the proper time for change!

83 If peace is indeed to succeed,
    the causes of discord must be reduced,
    especially injustice that results
        from economic inequalities,
        from a quest for power,
        or from contempt for personal rights.

84 The way to do this is for the human family
    sharing this planet together
    to create for itself a system of governance
        that is sufficient to meet the demands
        of these modern times.
We have the beginnings in current international agencies,
    and cooperation among all people,
        regardless of their religion,
        is central to this.
The Church is delighted with the growing
    cooperative spirit among nations
    both among Christians and non-Christians.

85 These international efforts should also be extended
    to the economic field
    where wealthy and developed nations
    assist others to procure the necessary material goods
        for a richer quality of life.
If this is to work, we will have to reduce
    excessive desire for profit,
    nationalistic pretensions,
    the lust for political domination,
    militaristic thinking,
    and schemes designed to promote ideologies.
86 Toward this end, we can offer some guidelines:
First, as nations develop
    they should strongly hold
    the complete human fulfillment of their citizens
        as the goal of their efforts.

Second, advanced nations have a heavy duty
    to assist developing people
    toward this end.
Third, the entire world should organize together
    to provide for economic growth
    but should do so taking into account
        the rights of all to determine their own fate
        and the duty of all to assist one another.
Fourth, there is a pressing need to reform
    the very structures of economic activity,
    but nations should be wary of solutions
        that nibble away at human spirituality
        or wholeness.

87 We do recognize the need in some places
    to regulate and reduce population growth.
Every effort should be made to distribute food and goods
    more fairly to all
    and, indeed, to increase production when possible.
And since so many people are concerned today
    about controlling population growth,
    we urge that whatever steps are taken
        be in accord with moral law.
The question of how many children a couple should have
    is a matter of conscience
    and not of government-imposed rules.
This parental decision takes into account
    educational and social conditions
    and these modern times.
People should be made aware in a wise manner
    of scientific advances that can help them
    arrange the number of their children.
The reliability of such methods should be proven,
    and they should be in harmony with our ethics.

88 Given all we have said,
    let us add that Christians also have a duty

to support personally those who are poor.
Certain wealthy nations, with mainly Christian populations,
    must become aware of the deprivation of other nations,
        the torment,
        disease,
        and hunger in the rest of the world.
Well-organized efforts to share resources
    should be undertaken,
    ecumenically when possible,
        to alleviate suffering everywhere.
As was true in the early years of the Church,
    Christians should meet the needs of these poor
    out of their own subsistence
        and not only from what is "left over."
Collections among Christians should be taken
    throughout the entire world
    in cooperation, when possible,
        with other Christians.

89 The Church stands among the nations
    as a catalyst of this activity.
To achieve this, the Church must be present
    among the nations
    in a thoroughgoing way,
        both through her members
        as well as institutionally.
90 Toward this end, we at this council
    now recommend the establishment of an agency
        of the universal Church.
This agency will have the task of promoting justice,
    stimulating the Catholic community to participate
    and work for social justice
        on an international level.
It will take its place among other agencies
    and help end the terrible hardships
    felt by people around the world today.

BREAKING OPEN THE CONCLUSION
(ARTICLES 91–93)

The tremendous task of Christians is to introduce love to the world. The example of Christ energizes our mission to serve the people of the modern world.

Part A

Read this conclusion aloud one article at a time, pausing to complete the discussion in Part A. As you read, underline key passages. Talk together about the elements that you noticed.

For instance, read article 92 and discuss: How does your parish foster mutual esteem, reverence, harmony, and the full recognition of legitimate diversity?

Conclude Part A by discussing: How do you go about fostering the above realities in your daily contacts?

Part B

When you have completed Part A, go on to discuss these questions:

How are Christians introducing love into the world?

How can various church denominations cooperate more in serving the people of the world?

PARAPHRASE TEXT

Conclusion

91 These proposals, dealing with many modern challenges,
    are meant for all people,
    whether or not they believe in God.
What we have said here is very general
    but it is rooted in the Gospel,
    and we hope further development
        of these ideas
        will produce action.

92 Indeed, the Church itself is a sign of cooperation
    based on honest dialogue.
This requires that we ourselves foster within the Church
    mutual esteem,
    reverence,
    harmony,
    and the full recognition of legitimate diversity.
We embrace those not yet in full communion with us
    to whom we are linked by faith
    and a common bond of charity.
Likewise, we embrace those who do not believe in Christ
    who also await unity and peace.

We fervently wish to have a frank conversation
    with all people of goodwill,
    everyone who seeks goodness and truth,
        excluding no one,
        even those who hate the Church,
            so we can build peace with all.

93 There is nothing, in short,
    for which Christians yearn more
    than to serve the people of the modern world
        generously and effectively.
We Christians shoulder a gigantic task
    which is to introduce love into the world,
    that love which we receive ourselves from Christ.
May Christ be with us in our work!